RISKING

AND

RUNNING

Poems
by
Lyle Crist

Pale Horse Press

1987

A number of poems in this collection have appeared in other publications, including the Lake Superior Review, Hiram Poetry Review, Good Reading, Sunshine Magazine, Creative Review, Western Ohio Journal, the English Journal, Sunstone Review, Ideals, First Bouquet, Having Writ, Runaways, Pudding, and Sunrust. "Tesseract", "Butterfly" and "Summer" are reprinted by permission from the Christian Science Monitor, © 1976, 1970, and 1986: "Before the Dawn" and "Fruitage" by permission of the Christian Science Sentinel, © 1976 and 1986. All rights reserved.

Sketches by Rachel Crist Nelson

ISBN 0-914-720-07-4

You remember what happens, your reactions, your curiosities. And you put these on paper. While you're at it, you consciously place into the writing a few of the basics-- some rhyme, alliteration, some metaphors, novel word usage, some rhythm. Most of all, you try to capture the awareness or intrigue which dominated your thought. Maybe the result is poetry.

Lawrence Ferlinghetti said that any poet is "constantly risking absurdity," peforming as an acrobat does on the high wire of the poet's choosing. But the poet is aware that at any time the audience may react the wrong way...also that the poet may plunge. The show may not be what the performer had planned.

Paul Williams told me that one trying to write creatively is in the same circumstance as a runner on third base in a baseball game. You're the runner; you think you can steal home -- and if you succeed, you're a hero. If you fail, you're a bum. An interesting comparison.

From a career in teaching college students, from family, from travel, from observations, interpretations, and speculations the poems in this collection have come. Maybe you'll take a seat and watch ... watch the acrobat and the ball player. And you can see whether there's any flair in my risking and in my running.

Lyle Crist

3

NATURE

PEOPLE

4

5

NATURE

SCENE AT DUSK

With the quilt of farm
on either side of road,
alone, I weave a quiet journey;
see the sheen of obedient cattle
lining home from forage
in the duskglow,
the first star opening.
I see the proud silhouettes
of thrusting silos,
see the dip and roll of land
fade as night appears.
I have not known these before,
yet each around—the field,
the herd, the farm—
bring remembrance of other times.

We link all to ourselves
in discerning what these are;
beauty, design, duty,
in field, in farm, in star.

FLIGHTS OF BIRDS

Against the
striations--
clouds fronting the glow
of dawn--
they sweep in communal cadance,
a frolic giving change
to the morning tapestry.

Is it merely exercise? A flexing
to signal the day's foragings?
Or early test of loyalty--
the flock in constant harmony
of wind and wing?
Or is it joyous celebration?

Sun rises, the stretching lines give way
and, so, my heart in
being part of this artistic scene--
whatever it may mean.

REMINDERS

In autumn,
when the maples and birches
scatter their russet and tawny selves
the pale meadows stiffen
through sharp and burnished days;
stoics, standing resolute;
firm reminders
of the need to
gird ourselves as well
when hard decisions come
in the seasons of our thought.

CAMPSITE MORNING

Against the patch of dawn
a lone bird
sits on the
mast of a shrub,
surveying
the curious movement
of campsite breakfast;
black sheen of wings
against the spreading light.
Then he rises
like the sun itself
which hurries
to blazon the canyon walls
in time to frame the flight,
the tapestry complete.

And we the morning gallery.

SYMPHONY AT CAPE MAY

The moment you reach
the porch
the overture begins;
the day's melody
in morning cadence
of the water violins.

Andante
The swells,
perceptible only as
brief shadings
of the ringlet sun,
soothe the heart, the stage
in rich deep—reed assurances;
tuneful corrugations,
parallel lines on the lyric page.

Allegro
Wind baton giving impetus,
cymbals crash and race
against the shoreline rocks,
spur the pace;
the music rushes in percussion pulse,
the trombone of the wind
giving insistent chase.

Moderato
Now with rise and fall,
now the motion arcs
across the vibrant floor
in rhythmic pronouncements
and modulated stance;
the harps in repetition,
the strum of the whitened crests,
refrain of ocean dance.

Finale
All now combine
in frolic surge of sound;
the porch audience approves,
the clapping of their hands remind
in nodding chorus--
the waves responding in their kind.

Joyous ocean melody the cause
of audience and ocean in mutual applause

BUTTERFLY

Dancing first.
Not fluttering, however much
it has been said.
Dancing.
There are, of course,
other accomplishements:
they may appear as nothing more
than aimless flag-flitting
but there is
placing,
testing,
nimble, hesitant, wingtip touchings,
antennae ferretings,
monarchial musings,
and wispy leg clutchings.
First, though,
dancing.

COTSWOLD GARDEN

Such glory! Bursts of red and gold
that overflow the tiny space,
spilling bounty on rock ledges,
filling views in floral grace.

The very smallest, the thimble plots,
boast petunias, asters, roses;
perky blossoms in ample clusters
striking happy poses.

With such expressions at these doors--
patchwork rainbows that one finds--
I know something of those inside,
the green leaves and blossoms of their minds.

THOUGHT AT OCEANSIDE

No man can measure ocean pulse
that sounds upon the granite coast;
rebuke of ocean calculus
each perfect wave is nature's boast.

Numbered peaks speak to me
I count the sediment of time.
Confused, I halt at ocean shore;
the throb of wave exceeds design.

FOREST PINES

New green at branch ends
like lessons learned
draw thought to
spires of mottled green
leaping in
the mountain crowd.
These pines know not retreat.
They teach persistence,
purpose,
patience.

POINT OF VIEW

This young polka-dot robin
that paused on green rim of stone bath
deciding, head cocked in searching,
did not know how much I hoped.
For him it was cleansing ritual considered,
but my moment hung as I waited
and watched his eyes as he debated.
Then he plunged
and I reveled in his ordered ways;
beak under, then forward thrust, and up
and on to rim, the preening, layering back
the folds, feather engines whirring.

What was this affirmation? You may ask:
for him it was merely a needful task
of body, made in routine measure;
for me it was insight, knowledge, pleasure.

TWILIGHT IN THE PETRIFIED FOREST

Blinking amber eyes,
day gives way to night
while these
amethyst-fed logs
bedded here
since antiquity
grace in patient pose.

Quietness spreads
across the park
punctuated not by sound
but only
by the cones, hillocks,
and blunt mesas afar.

In stillness
the work goes on,
ageless trends,
the coming together.
Beauty's quiet labor,
the hidden song.

THE SANDIA MOUNTAINS
ABOVE ALBUQUERQUE

Like snow-crested sentries
they loom at urban rim
with strata lines suggesting
now a smile
now a frown.
Looking on the town
they critique
in judgment from floor to peak;
these sentries, dutiful parents
judge the sprawling progress
of their lower forms.

SHELLS

One walks on shattered fragments
on ocean shores, some like knives
that years ago in ocean depths
held gelid forms of lives.

Sand misleads; its tumbled texture--
smooth to simple sense--
is bearded, each single, broken shard
is mute evidence

that these all served as fate's boundries;
not bones nor fleshy kind,
but fluted architecture, channeled limits,
straggled bits, that now remind

we walk on what the oceans attest;
numberless ways of life, now manifest.

WILDERNESS ENCOUNTER

We were both curious --
the boaters and the lone deer
that foraged
at rim of water.

Between green spears
that danced in the morning breeze
the deer peered, head a-tilt;
we, the intruders, pointing
and picturing.
At four arms' length
we appraised,
each at each,
till satisfied, our curiosities
retreated, found again
in evening conversation,
grins, and happy recallings.

Perhaps the deer, too,
smiled, and
told the others.

ASPEN

Like
dangling earrings
from countless stem-lobes,
the leaves frolic
on bouncing winds.

If my line of thought
is right,
the aspen
hears more
than any other
forest tree.

CHIPMUNK LEAVES

Obedient to the wind
bristling about the yard
to meeting places
in corners, backs of trees;
mounding till the
wind changes its mind
adjourning heaps.

TO THE DRIFTWOOD

How far have you come?
Shard of time, remnant of some
long journey's ocean quest;
part of a mast, perhaps; the rest
along this rim of sand and shell
all have, as you, tales to tell.
But of your lonely past -- where and why?
It was a water's lullabye
that rocked you, moved you to this place,
your time set in crested pace.
Were you across the bay? Beyond?
Whether from ocean span or coastline pond
the pulsing waves have fashioned you --
gentle strokes of them accrue
and leave a kind of silent sheen
belying age, unwrinkled, clean.
Your journey's end, shard of time,
now becomes a part of mine.

ENGLAND, LAKE COUNTRY

The heathered hills, the heaves of earth
that contour lives; no dearth
of theme or focus when
one seeks to use a poet's pen.

Brief clusters of the homes and barns,
the song of bird, the sheen of tarns,
the sheep upon the endless rise
and fall of land, the treasured skies
in changing loom, the threads of roads
in open fields -- such goads
make harvest for a poet's mind
to prosper thought, spur it to find
the flat block stones that long ago
were set in rigid paths that sew
the fabric of these hills, the coverlet
that settles gently. I have a debt
that weighs upon the words I choose:
to share the bounty of these views.

SQUIRREL AND TAIL

Duty? Perhaps it was
as they moved across the lawn
towards some purpose beyond my view.

It was the sequence I absorbed:
one gray squirrel, yet two in flight
for his body-long duster tail, not upright
nor arrowed
was coursing in slow arcs
with each lope—spring, hurtle, descent—
patterning exactly the
body sweep
and, so, two curves.

Sequential harmony.

Duty? Or was is structure?

But a jet's contrails are of different
substance,
a cat's tail is like a flag,
the wake of boat hunts shore on
either side,
and a mouse merely drags his.
Was it habit?
This rhythmical, squirrel-tail curve?
Like a child playing house
imitating the elder body
it was
and I followed
both in each,
this cadenced undulating.

Now, recalling the beauty of
the parent leap
I say perhaps it was
neither duty
nor habit
nor yet structure
that spurred this
dual ribboning.

Perhaps
it was admiration.

RIVER CONVERSATION

The cadenced conversation
of the river--
like some club meeting,
the flowing words,
the different voices
petulant at times,
or demanding;
phrases swirling
around the canyon room.
Now some echo
brought up again,
the river
speaking in
fluid tongue, the
meeting adjourning
to the
conversation of the seas
beyond
my view.

BEFORE THE DAWN

Before the dawn
the song began.
Before the sweep of light
—no matter if it was moments or more—
this backyard bird
sang, knowing;
his melody a harbinger.

And I thought
how often
only after rewards were given
have I sung;
but how
faith is a song

before the dawn.

THE PEACE ROSE

Within the folds the message grows;
within the beauty of the rose.
From merest stem and simplest form
through springtime sun and summer storm
the silent melody of love's endeavor
is seen in tiny folds that never
cease to fulfil a kind
of joyous message to receptive mind.
They move in plan that always settles
in fuller view, in broadening petals.
like the joy of widening thought
that blossoms forth in lessons taught!
Beauty is within, to be understood
as we nurture it in brotherhood
for within its folds, nature knows
the triumphant peace seen in the rose.

SUMMER STATUE

Alone
in layered July heat
that sears the mesa,
this horse has
no desert shrub
to shadow him.
Time of impreceptible
motion
or, at most, muted cadence.

He has learned his lesson
and
statue-like
he stays
until the sky will deepen.
Even a blush will do.

PELICAN

On constant winds he sweeps
across white sand manor
at water's edge,
splits silent currents
with long beak prow,
then with lancet wings
that end in fringe.

Pulsing wings,
he descends to ocean's peak,
beauty of the flight
acknowledged
in surfaced offerings
and in cadenced clapping
of the waves.

TEMPERING

The gull along the restless shore
stood on one leg; I saw no more.
What had prompted such a stance?
He moved then, in a kind of dance
that was no pose for other birds,
his look at me was beyond words;
smug, he slowly unwound his limb—
it jacknifed in poetic hymn
that suggested joy to me
and more — it was his victory.
I suspect now my point is made:
in all my time to promenade
I could never retract, tuck a leg in
under my wrinkled stomach skin.
He was beyond me; as it unwound
I merely watched, and then I frowned
and as he sauntered off on two
I heard him laugh; well, such things accrue—
there is a tempering in being aware
through the things we see, the things we bear.

ON THE NATURAL DEATH OF BIRDS

Do the small talons merely
arc slowly,
leaving brief lines
against the limbs
before the plummet
to oblivion?
Or is it bare forkings
in settled dirt—
merely a slow cadence
into leafed burial,
soft closing?
Is this how the lofty bird dies?

Rapid eyes cutting through
green leaf bosom of trees,
then the confident
pulsing
of dominion again:
oh, I have seen them!
Scoriating skies in
thrusted beauty!

But what of the final moment,
the ended flight?
Last burst of wind and wing?

WHO DECIDES?

You've seen them?
Rippling blankets,
clusters of birds
that from their forages
unison to the air in
vibrant, communal sweeps?
How is the leader known?
What mystique of call decides?

The morning moves over me.
What is known, what I touch,
I understand.

Only what is known,
only what I touch.

LINES IN THE MORNING

Early morning slate air
at Kansas farm;
black steer glisten,
unwinding in long procession
from barn to prairie.
They weave in obedient lines
toward pasture, rhythmic time
of hoof, nose, trunk in slow rolls.

I think of
parades
and school children
and political parties,
of circus entrances,
of elephant walk,
red ants,
whistle of steel mill,
and of families.
Of celebration
of the new day.

LESSON

I am told that birds
stake out territories,
establish grassy areas of their own;
their songs from slender branches
more than mere tunes
so that "nothing inappropriate"
(a fieldguide phrase)
may enter here.

I must leave you now
applying what I've been taught—
to climb the
branches of my thought.

BLEA TARN, CUMBRIA

Seeing all this
one thinks in studied shame
of castles, the shallow thrusts
of briefest fame, the
patterned ways, the homes,
the steepest spires
and fashion domes;
for here at quiet mountain lake
nature and mankind forsake
the lofted stones and pagentry--
well intended as they might be--
and in rustic beauty yet unbroken
bring instead the deepest token
God has sought;
the quiet offering of lofted thought.

SUMMER

I have seen summer
squeeze its way through door cracks
and then another year burst in
vibrant sunrise thought.
It is coy again, leaving only
hints at the doorstep:
brief tan, momentary mist on forehead.
Again, it is open—
the assured rabbit by the azalea --
or it is the day unwilling to
trade place with the night.
Another year it may wait, hesitant
to be seen
as though it arrived
ahead of the mail.
It is sure by the calendar
but delight is not in sureness.
The joy is in how
summer itself chooses
to let me know.

WHY THE TREE SHED ITS LEAVES

It was practical
planning,
why the tree
shed its leaves,
dropped its leafy garment
in autumnal ritual
and now stands naked --
knowing well that
as it preens itself
by winter's mirror
it will grow,
fatten limbs, take another notch
in girth of trunk.

When April comes, the maple knows,
it needs a larger suit of clothes.

SUCH ACTIVITY

Just beneath the
foam of clouds
they came--
the squadron of geese in
lofted formation,
with yet a smaller contingent--
perhaps ten or so--
within the Vee;
persistent tenor trumpet call
urging the cadenced wings.

Is the sequence by chance
or by assignment?
And those inside--
are they the favored ones?
The elder? The more cautious?

The sweep fades,
cloud caressed,
my questions now just
a source of gratitude.

PEOPLE

FLOWER PEOPLE

In yard patches of city slopes—
ragged, green remnants of wilderness hopes—
mid belching chimneys; between these vaults
one finds in such desperate faults
that contrast persists and sometimes unfolds
in yellow and orange of wild marigolds.

How right each time that sorrow's chains
are severed by those who stake out claims
on something beyond this pitiful scene,
rooted, instead, in brief wisps of green.

So, one must make choices, and usually holds
to people who persist—like marigolds.

IN TARRYTOWN

Here,
with trees shrouding
the house
he named Sunnyside,
I can see the Hudson
in nature's frame.
I think of the people
he placed
in these same
mountain troughs:
Ichabod and Brom,
Katrina, Wouter von Twiller,
and Rip.
The morning warmth gives rise to my quiet smile.

Once
Washington Irving
stood here,
lank as the trees,
confident as the river flow.
In this moment
I am aware that
he, too,
on this very spot,
may have thought
of Ichabod and Brom,
Katrina and Wouter von Twiller,
and Rip --
and he may have smiled, as I,
quietly.

NOW AND ONCE

Almost antiseptic,
the garage this Saturday.
He moves in ordered paths, no need
for the broom, in place
against the wallboard,
its fringed comb
unwearing.

Saturdays once were taxing;
the kid's bikes, wagon, the
catcher's mitt and bat thrown.
It took half a day
to bring respectability
with hula hoops, wire coils
for rabbit hutch, the football,
pogo sticks, skates
in hurried heaps.

Hovering,
the muted neatness
and on the sheen of a recent shelf,
once playhouse siding,
his hand searches,
pulsing, like the
pendulum
of the clock on kitchen wall.

TWO PICTURES FROM POMPEII

I

"Approaching next, on your left the
classic ruins of
the Temple of Jupiter
with remnants of the
public meeting area."
He put the guidebook away;
"Better move along, Martha."
Next, fishing out camera
from enormous bag
he adds,
"Sure looks old, huh? Over
there, Martha! Now, smile—
the bus is waiting."
Such talk for marble clusters,
timeless drapery
for her quick
and meaningless face!

AT THE FORUM

II

"Get away from
that pillar, Henry
it looks like
it'll fall over
any minute!"

BRIEF MEETING
BY ELEVATOR

Volcano hair erupted in streaks
segments pouring about her wan cheeks.
I watched as she stood by elevator,
spindle-heeled rising, and later
poufed, pomaded,
flowered yet faded
she was, behind saucer-sized glasses.
I made no passes.
Her desperate advertising campaigns
now underway were--like all such
claims--
exaggerated, taking many chances,
as she waited and hoped for glances
and opportunities and even more,
opening like the elevator door.

Being one who knows that he cares,
I felt sorry. And then took the stairs.

FOR DICK KINNEY

Neither sounds of children nor traces of the light;
gone the vibrant whispers, the melodies of being,
pictures of the day's bright seeing
in sensed patterns of the world. Delight
in all of these deprived. Lost each detail
of others, knowing scenes, sounds; the paradigm
of expectations of life, unknown to him
who lives in vacuum's eternal veil.

Yet the star, not knowing darkness, still gleams;
in its own brilliance its world is infinite,
and love itself is unaware of opposite,
They persist for what they are, not what seems
and where they are, the want, the void
is not the vital stress
and where the mind persists, there is no less
than all to be discerened, enjoyed.

For him life's grand fruition overflows
in family, his school, his mission fraught
with touch and taste, remembered thought;
serenely he shares a life's rainbows.
No mourning! To sorrow's deep chagrin
judgment's message transcends all doubt;
it is not what he is without —
it is what he is, within.

THE CASTLE BUILDERS

Forgotten,
those who toiled
the endless days
to loft these walls on
the gnarled land.
The endless tapestries,
the full-wall portraits
poses of the regal.
But for those
who toiled,
the pictures only
in the lofted stones, the
walls, the interplay of
the ground and stone.

PARADOX

Out on the terrace she welcomes the sun,
exposes arms, legs, face until done;
stretched on chaise lounge rotisserie
she bakes, endures such hot misery;
avoids a burn with lotioned skill
and seeks, instead, deep tan until
against darkest tone she clothes in white
and ventures forth into the night.

Friends applaud her skin and her gown:
"My dear, you're absolutely brown!"
This song of praise prompts her quick smile,
her oven hours well worth the trial.
She nods, and conversation passes
to matters of the lower classes.
She says, "I'm appalled at how they act;
they're retrograde -- and it's a fact,
you know, they all live in sin --
you can tell by the color of their skin!"

EGO—DRIVER

He will not stop at red lights,
but intent upon being himself
and having the world know this
fact
he leaves behind
the statutes, dusty documents,
the courthouse catacombs
and turns, instead, to
leaping intersections,
jaywalking the car;
bolting past the
light which blinks
in disbelief.

The car wears its bruises well—
mangled fender, pinched door,
under-plumbing askew from
crossroad buffeting.

But his lonely self,
the assertion,
the purposed ego,
is untouched,
missed by all the crowd.

PRECISELY

"You do not understand," they say on campus,
the intent ones, with manuals and guides.
"You are too old. You do not understand
love, today."

I who teach Dickinson who knew its silence.
I who teach Fitzgerald who thought it less than wealth.
I who teach Whitman who thought of little else than love.

"You are not the one to learn from," they say.
"You are gray and white and tell the same stories
from class to class and you are not at our parties.
What do you know of love today?"

What else can a man tell but of his own --
of worth, of hope, of love?
And they ask, mocking, as they leave,
"Which manual did you use? And did you have
expert counseling?"

And I say, "One day I was crying and someone touched my hand
and looked at me and then I did not cry."
And the students pause, "You mean you cried with tears?
A man with tears down his face?"
One asks, "Was it an accident?"
That is what they think. That is what they think it is.
I say, "There were no tears at all."
The young ones stare. "But you told us you were crying."
Again I say I was. "But it is inside, with no tears
or sobs at all."

And they say, in triumph,
"You do not make sense, old man."
They turn to leave with knowing glances. "How did she
know you were crying
if there were no tears
and if there were no sobs at all?"

And I say,
"Ah, my young friends, that is precisely what love is."

OLD WOMAN

Her hand showed network
of veins,
abundant as the wire mesh
of cart
she dragged along
the narrow walk
while mouthing conversations to herself.
I will avoid this;
she is no part of me.
She stared in antique store window
looking at dusty book, the crooked table,
faded chair and ottoman —
seeing nothing but herself.
Jolting again, she
approached me;
I would have chosen the street,
but race of cars kept me near;
I could feel the ragged membrane of
her coat
as we passed;
a contagion,
plague.
Frantic, I sought to brush it off,
every vistage of the touch of this
old-woman dirt;
and sweep of arm drew me to my own
hand,
to my own veins,
more than I had ever noticed
before.

JUNIOR HIGH

Thirteen, perhaps; he pauses with
studied manner
out of NBC, pulls a filter king from
rain jacket, lets it suspend
from pursed lips
dried by autumn winds.
It is seven forty-five;
junior high home room soon.
Blue shirt, tail out, tight chinos,
uncombed hair, meager lunch held loosely,
he leans forward,
draws ashes into the filter king
till countdown ends
(I am in the car at the light, reading
the intersection)
and ignition completes this
public coupling.
Then he becomes another early morning
chimney
along with U.S. Steel.
Flicking, then hunching,
he walks on,
inhaling visions of all the tablet of manhood:
conquest, adoration, virility, ease.
Visions against a cold, blue morning.
Pulp paper targets along the rifle range.

SHE SITS ALONE

She sits alone
mid the celebrants,
those moving in the
corporate lines;
the fireplace flames
of suburban house
(the patterned stones
surrounding)
as consistent as the talk --
incessant talk --
of drink and party,
last week's binge
after hours.
The records set.

Scattered among the
laughing plaudits,
the other wives respond on cue,
giggle at the accounts
but
among the colored stones
(her head down
in focussed purpose)
she rubs her fingers
in nervous lines
across each other,
feigning interest,
as though discovering
something important
in the
shallow folds.

HONEYMOONERS
AT THE MOTEL

Arm in arm they go
their morning now the afterglow
of their celebration night.
I watch them stroll, this youthful sight.
Her levis are a pristine white,
in retrospect so very tight —
the pattern of her body mold
in lucid movement, delicious, bold.
One sees magnetic, supple lines
which by her clothes are more defined.
If she were in these arms of *mine*
I would — well, at any rate,
I, too, would celebrate.

THE HUNTER

Did you hear his defense?
His reasoned plea?
"They would die of starvation
if we did not hunt.
We keep them from the
pain, the agony
of cold winter death,"
he says.

Show me one hunter
who kills not
for the kill itself.
Show me one hunter who
rises at dawn to comb the battled fields,
to stalk the forest ridge
till scent and leap and cry —
for mercy's sake alone.

Show me one.

CYNIC'S VIEW

In wheelchair she sold candy boxes
mid-sidewalk, smiling
for those leaving the bank.
Swathed, turbaned, gloved
in winter's frigid breath,
she offered them in warmth
of endeavor, her smile genuine--
if, indeed, the chair was needed.

At rim of interstate
he stood.
His open hand in hesitant gesture.
Constant rain veiled my view
but his honest movement
showed the need for borrowed ride--
if, indeed, the gesture was unrehearsed.

At the register
she ran tired fingers,
pressed the tally keys,
then said, "Have a nice day."
The sackful of items processed,
arranged, dealt with mechanically
on contrast to her
caring self--
if, indeed, the words were not packaged, too.

LIFE ALONG THE TIDAL ZONE

Tod the tadpole lived in a tide pool
but Tad the toad lived on a toadstool.
Though Tod learned to swim at the tide school
Tad kept away, as a general rule.
Things just work out, they are really great
for Tod and Tad, but I can't keep them straight--
looking for a toad pad in a tad pole
or is it a tide stool on a toad pole?
I mean, Toad Tad keeping cool
in the tide ... oh! what a fool!
Is it a toad pod who rules on a stool?

I'd better go back to the tide school.

THE STORAGE

If I could turn around and gather in my arms
the souvenirs of other days, the charms,
the toys, the games, and the hats,
the ticket stubs, the fielder's glove, the baseball bats,
the furniture, the cars, the fashions, and the faces,
the rooms and windows, and all the places --
I'd put them in a storage box
with heavy sides and several locks
and, re-living times, I'd reach in
to what I'd call my "where I have bin"!

SERYOUS POEM

Ah, docile tragedy
how you wait in turgid frome.
Ah, silent wave unleashed --
waif among the sands!
Ah, ego of the hours!
Ah, dauntless chiliarch!
Ah, yet the murmur of the flute
and who frets?
Ah, needless weave of time
that moves motionless!
Ah, steadfast pursuit
of the immovable yet
the sandpiper grows.
Ah, warm enfolding!
Ah, morning savour!
Ah, phooey.

CREST OF SNOW

The crest of snow
looms mightily after winter storm;
like some mighty monarch
it arches against the sky.

Then the wind swirls around it,
picks up the fluffy white hill
and disperses it.

Should we say
it now appears crestfallen?

TO OUR OLD
ELECTRIC MIXER

I like the clatter
of the batter
in the beater;
thought it's neater
if the latter
doesn't splatter,
yet the pounding
of its sounding
though it's frightful
is delightful
for the clutter
of the butter
in the beater
is much better
than the clitter
of a fritter
getting fatter
in its batter
when the matter
in the beater
finds my platter.

Who can utter
words to flatter
better than a beater?

What is sweeter
for an eater
but the chatter
of the batter
in the beater?

THREE GIFTS

There were three of them on this Christmas day
Merv was the one who would obey
the manger scene of child -- a way
of love for all, divine display.

Goldie was next, a girl who knew
the promise, who found she grew
in faith that would imbue
the Christ, so joyous and so true.

The third was Frank who in reverence
felt that God's omnipotence
impelled him -- well, in a sense --
to be an example, love's evidence.

"They had gifts?" some would discuss.
"Something of glory, the fabulous?"
The three said, "We give ourselves, our impetus
to share God's love through each one of us."

That night they say their magic gifts
helped all in love the Christ child to serve:
the boundless way of gifts that were
Goldie, Frank (in sense), and Merv.

SUPPERTIME

What joy it is to nibble
on the fruition
of labors in the kishun!

GUISEPPE

There is a starling
feeding on my
backyard perch.

This dark, sleek bird
is named Guiseppe.
He flew here
from Milan,
has rested on the leaning tower,
spends most summers
near Naples,
and enjoys
fettuccini and
riccotta cheese as well.

I know all this
because
he is eating
pizza crumbs
in the backyard feeder.

DEER ONE

The doe broke through the deep green bush
at last it did appear;
I aimed the camera, then gave a push,
and said, "Thanks much! You're such a deer!"

TEACHING

PROFESSOR'S CLASSROOM SCENE
--THE EXAMINATION--

Whether caught by window's sheen
or inside the hand, barely seen,
the furrows on each studied brow
mark this time, I see them now

with pens above the pages, and texts
spread across the narrow desks --
full spectrum of the colors brought
and spectrum, too, of range of thought.

I know the wisdom they bring to this
with mind and pen, the synthesis
to bring to light intelligence...
and I await the evidence.

FOR MAY DAY

Take the beauty of this summertime day in May,
and fling it around a star in wondrous display;
I would take the meaning of the moment here
and wrap it in satin, its lustered art revere;
for I would hold the sweet flavor of campus youth
revealing itself in some springtime truth
as in the wonder now of May's bud and blooms
as flowers open doors to their petaled rooms.
One flower, one youth gives stars, satin, flavor sublime.
I will remember, I will hold this treasured time
in thought, radiant as nature's sweet countenance
mirrored in your faces, this day's benevolence.

PROF AND STUDENT

Have you ever seen a prof
when his dignity is off?
With his classroom air all shot
now that everything's been taught?
Shoes off, bad joke, peanut butter,
evening paper, crazy dreams, fix the shutter,
television, Saturday bath, atom bomb,
Dr. Pepper, bank book balance, note to Mom,
chase the dog, clean your room, many meetings,
on the phone, off to church, and Christmas greetings,
cheese sandwich, love, pleased, and worried,
ping pong, model cars, and always hurried,
heartaches, glories, bit of fame:
prof or student — much the same.

PEDAGOGUE

Ipso facto and *sina quo non* and thus so *cum laude;*
I consider myself an authority of *op cit*
as well.
Magnum opus and *ergo*
go nicely with *et al* as well.
If A then not B
ergo.
Proviso and compendium and let it be known
ipso facto magna cum note card
it is *per quod* because *ergo* is *ergo.*
Ah! A square ergo!
Hypotenuse, Decartes, Pythagoras, factotum
and when in the course
of human events it becomes
necessary
that unless and wherefore
it is not to be unconsidered
inconsequential
ibid ibid ibid
ibid ibid
ibid.

LITERATURE PROF

The text had 187 short stories
and two cartons of poems
and a full index
(and there was something more than a
hundred pieces of asphalt tile on the
floor in the room; I started counting them
one day)
—as I said, there were 287
short stories and three cartons
of poems
or whatever the number was and
I spent most of my time
trying to show them what makes a story
click,
a poem
mean something
and I said, "See the cycle of events
and we begin where we end and
we see the use of setting in 'Open Boat'
by Crane because the sea is unsafe and
land is security
and all four men must move from
danger to safety
and that is good use of setting.

And look at the richness of simple
reference in
Frost's 'Axe-Helve'. Imagine! A man
spending his life molding axe-helves!
But he knows there is a right helve for
each man and that, I submit,
is rich use of simple reference.
That is what I mean."
Pry open minds, wedge wisdom
so that they can see *for themselves* how it is
with literature.

Well, with 387 short stories and
four cartons of poems in our text
we finished, followed syllabus, and so
it was examination time and I asked
all that I could ask:

"From 487 short stories and five cartons
of poems, discuss use of cycle in stories,
tell me about useful setting, describe some
simple poetic reference that is rich
in universal meanings."

And paper and paper and paper and paper
came in for grading and they say,
"See! How well we know our lesson." They write,
"See the cyclic effect in the Trilling story,
the cycle ends where it has begun and what
better setting could there be than land
and sea in 'Open Boat' for here
the sea is danger and land is safety;
how useful; how appropriate it is!"
They say, "And there is no better poetry of
simple reference than 'Axe-Helve' for
here is a man dedicated to molding an
axe-helve to the man, spending his life
to the proposition!"
And the papers summarize, "Truly this course
has given me wisdom and understanding and
awareness, for now I can discern what
literature is and I am much better for having
been in your class."

I am desolate,
but, with 587 short stories and six cartons
of poems in the text, nicely indexed,
I must meet another class next term.
Ah! I am afraid that soon I shall
do no more
than count the tiles
on the floor.

NEW STUDENT

To the Pretty Young Coed
in Freshman English, the
Opening Day of School

> Fair Hair
> but
> Fear Here

TEACHER

Lives, not mere faces,
are in
classroom rows,
though impatience,
despair, sullen view
interposing
would have this
unremembered.
Chalkboards express disciplines
in hourly cadence.
Teachers show remembrances.

CREATIVE WRITING CONFERENCE
MY UNDERGRADUATE DAYS

Each upward step
brought nearer the caustic word;
I could have avoided
his slateboard voice
spewing out criticisms
of my short stories--
yet I returned
each Thursday,
stalking to his cluttered
landing office in
University Hall.
Again, the tearing apart,
rending my soulwork.
Some kind of God he was
in high heaven
and I the fallen angel
my corruptions bared.
I in weekly penitance.

THE OPEN BOOK TEST

The sun that brief spring afternoon
rose cheerless over the students of doom.
Through custom, obedience they had now been lured
into the classroom, their fate now assured.
for it was an open book test! it had all seemed so easy!
But then why were the students all quiver and queasy?
The answer was clear; it was the olde prof at fault
who to all order and learning would now call a halt.
They'd studied Whittier, Holmes, and Thoreau
but deep in their hearts they all would know
that'd he'd ask trick questions that no one could handle!
They'd heard of his ways! Just right for a scandal!

And then they sat down, the awful test now at hand.
Three questions! Horrible! For none had they planned!
The terrible first was, "How many pages in the text?"
Oh, what kind of a deep question would he ask next?
Second: "who was the publisher?" Third: "How much did it cost?"
Oh! If only we'd prepared -- then not all would be lost!

Just those three questions, in an open book test!
Oh, how they struggled and all did their best
but they could not find one answer -- not one answer was there!
An open book test is too hard! It's not fair!

PRAYER FOR THE
NEW TEACHER

Now go forth
glowing
in God's intelligence,
sowing
the word of truth,
knowing
that every heart
responds
to that word,

and through that word
to your expression
as well.

ON HAVING READ THE PERFECT PAPER

Joy unbounded is mine today
I've given a theme a grade of A.
No participles dangled, no words misspelt.
It's the greatest joy I've ever felt!
Topic sentences, proper diction;
this sounds as though it must be fiction
but the words were there in right sequence.
Excellent expression! Some days hence
I'll put it back upon the shelf—
pretend I hadn't written it myself.

MOMENTS

FRUITAGE

As in the field
it is not merely the vast plans,
or the seeds themselves, the
fencing, the marking off
that brings the bounty --

it is the sowing.

So in our prayers
it is not the repetitions,
the word themselves, the
memorizing, the marking off of times --

it is the knowing.

PICTURE OF A
STARVING CHILD

No, I have not seen the
children, just pictures:
the war orphans,
the little hands reaching,
the desperate faces
of those outcast,
the crying babe mid the shelled
streets, the naked girl
fleeing napalm.
And
this starving one, the buttock-boy
astride some nameless, dirty road
in India, bones of legs askew,
his pitiful threads of arms
between,
propping the listless
oversize head.
Burden of skull
beyond the tragic arms.
What did he with camera do?
Lens rewards this moment
but I know—
so deeply etched within me the knowing-
beyond the distillation
of the photograph
the pitiful head moves closer
to the dirt.
I know it moves,
its last journey
defined in the
unfulfilled dream
that the child never knew
he had.

TURTLE

Raccoon carcass and rigid possum
no longer probing highways. I have seen;
and dogs, of course, jagged corpses.
Rabbits molded into turnpike by Goodyear
as ruts are patched.

I dislike this,
yet in distasteful contrasts
accelerating against remnants unmoving
we are made wise
and motion lured my eyes
on river road. No Mississippi current
or auto speed,
but this dim visage ahead, midway
in four lanes;
it becomes a turtle, six inches of shell
in breadth
in ponderous cadence.
I stop; we meet, his neck unwinding
from secret recess,
and confused, yet knowing, he turns away
as drivers behind me look
with disdain.

Frivolous act!

From them, not him, I move, my last view
indelible of him starting back
in face of traffic, head searching,
eyes high, wide feet thrusting against man.

He looks at me again. I shall
not forget his eyes.
he does not belong there on August concrete.

To comprehend it is to shun his heritage
and, driving on, like some sage
I knew his odds and wept alone.
His shell or cadence I have not known.
That slimy recess, that scaly skin—
these are things that are not akin.

to my own ways; yet I am wise
remembering now his high set eyes
which searched for some vain, hopeful clue,
unaware of roadside residue
but sensing danger, seeking home
he plodded. It was like some poem
leading to an awesome theme,
word by step in saddened scheme.
I could have saved him, I watched his head,
but concerned with impatience of cars instead
I left him, and now I thrust
my thoughts out warily, I must
beat against the traffic flow
and raise *my* head, for I know
few would understand these ties,
yet I am linked to him, his eyes
in that moment hunted love.

I cannot find myself above
that call, not in any guise.
I cannot now forget his eyes.

GIVING UP

Giving up, disposing of conclusions
that are, to you,
as sharp and known as
the conch, nail, sweet melon on the vine.
Giving up fragments or
whole selves:
love seems this way,
giving mind's shrugs,
the final nod, "All right, if you wish
it your way."

Gone the sunsets, valleys, quiet hands
and promises,
even more, the early flesh
Love discovers
beyond the touch and whim
a giving up,
as steel is tempered, the metal flexing
a sacrifice manifest always.

But not a losing.
If one thinks of defeats
discoveries persist.
It is a building
in hourly richness.

TESSERACT

(Theoretical four-dimensional figure)

The tesseract,
so purely logical,
raises issue.
If two points
make a line,
four lines a square,
six squares define a cube—
then, one is told,
eight cubes establish
the tesseract, enclosing,
defining.
I have the logic, yet
cannot view this, nor accept.
But I do know of a child's love,
dispelling rancor;
my brother's smile, lofting my heart,
hands enfolding where distance
once ruled:
from these, assurance
that others,
pyramiding love,
will establish, define
without limit.
I will hold to these.

Perhaps I will
return to the
tesseract
some other day.

ENCOUNTER IN THE MUSEUM

Billboard size,
this art work
consists of a rectangle
(in orangebrown; this must
be talent)
above smaller ones
(in orange and brown; this
must be talent).
All of which brings
awe
(at least to those who one day
in paneled rooms offered funds
for this work).

Down the corridor
the exit sign,
lush single lines,
one word
that insures order.
One rectangle,
one word.
(There must be talent).

READING POEMS

Reading poems for understanding
even aloud and
in studious need
we may find differences
of opinion.
It is like
you and I
being touched by the motion of the wind
across our faces
for unless our eyes are tuned,
our cheeks aligned,
nostrils exact
in catching the single current,
interpretations come.
Our faces are not one.
Yet winds need not distress;
for later
when the bird is silent
and the work of the breeze
is seen in tufts of leaves
and in settled lines
of dust against the window,
we talk about the wafted impress,
dimensions of the touch,
and find our heart's response.

It is then
we understand
the
differences.

CATCHING POEMS

Like swan wings
against the blue sky
the crests of lake
dance in whitened lines
to the tempo of the wind,
then push to scattered shore.

Poems are like this:
patterns formed
when winds of thought stir
the lines,
catching the idea that shimmers
in the moment's phrase.

They are always moving in our minds;
trumpeter wings that have caught
the ridge and flow of poetry
and lead to crested thought.

IT IS THE KIND

Perhaps you have noticed
dogs in parked cars.
The toy poodles scurrying
around in Imperials, Cadillacs,
and
the shepherds, the Great Danes
in red Volkswagons and
yellow Volkswagons
so hunched, arched
in forced roofline fancy,
their paws splattering over seats
with hardly enough room
for the driver.

Of the two, I've found
more room for love
in the latter,
the jeaned drivers grinning commands,
then the ready conversations of
runs and forages,
the tussles and the hearty holds —
while the others, in velour
with no place to jump
go nowhere in common ground
with their masters.
There is only "now, now, now"
and "no, no, no."

You and I
would gladly hunch
for such acceptance as some have.
It is not the size or space.
It is the kind of love.

INTERRUPTIONS

Interruptions!
Why, you have
no idea
what they can mean
until
you
have observed
the tireless
crow
working away
at some remnant
in the right-hand land
of
Interstate 80.

SEASHORE SCENE

Patchwork array,
of oceanside togs,
slatted chairs,
the games,
frantic weekend tanners,
the red and white
concession stands.
Against these
the straight crest lines
of timeless, ordered
ocean pulse.
The same if none were there
at all.

THE DIFFERENCE

Looking up
I found the stars in place
one ebon night.
It was faith that led.

Thick clouds were low
the next dark night
and though I could not see,
I knew the stars in place.

(Now understanding led, instead)
Through faith, the stars confirming;
through understanding,
I, affirming.

GETTING DOWN IN WEEDS

It's a right thing,
getting down in weeds
that catapult skyward
on their own
in vacant city lots
every summer.
Scraunch.
That's the word.
I'm not sure how to spell it
but I know what it means.
With your chin on the ground
the wind-swept fabric
of wild mustard or foxtail grass
is taller than the new bank
or the hamburger shack
or the Texaco sign,

And the point is
that
may really be the truth.

QUIET SANDALS

And love
in quiet sandals moves about,
stopping in deep moments
when we find each other.

Twos.
We revere twos,
one with one;
two fingers uplifted,
two hands entwined
(especially if yours and mine).

But if quiet sandals move on past—
the ones, still ones, now in contrast
wonder, is there the moment when
they will turn to us again?

REMEMBRANCE

There was Richard in World War Two and
we were
high schoolers together
and he has been gone a generation
and more.
It was a B-17 and it was 1942
and he did not want to go.
I wanted to go, but they took two inches
out of my hip when I was six.
He wanted debate team and school paper
and scholar's books
but there are ten men in a Flying Fortress
and they march with songs of
the wild blue yonder,
like teams bursting through
stadium tunnel,
hearts high as goal posts
and the B-17 opens its insides and
they become part.
"Gear switch."
"Neutral."
"Turbos."
"Off."
"Cabin heat."
"Ready."
"Starting engines!"
Engines alive and you feel spine prickles
and the plane is a living thing and you are
a part of it and a pelican is not meant
to stand always on weathered posts
jutting at water's edge by docks
and a comorant is top heavy and awkward on soil
and the eagle is in cumbersome swagger
at roadside
but when these go aloft
rightness comes

and now you are going to be right and you
say, "Brakes."
"Open."
"Trim tabs."
"Set."
"Generators."
"Checked."
And the throttle moves and the bird moves
and I have known this young man in study
hall, who did not want to fly
and I did want to fly
and I memorized every part
of the B-17
(and the language)
but Richard flew it, not I,
over Italy,
dropping eggs
and it was shot down in a February
splintered wing, rudderless, crippled bird
agonizing,
vomiting ten crew men in wasted residue
and I knew his death
even as I knew my own.
His came flying this bird-plane in clouds
aloft, in flight;
and mine came in emptiness of soil
and in weathered post
and still in cumbersome swagger.

GAPS

Time passes
like wisps of clouds
across the face of the moon
and
only occasional gaps
make awareness
of backwards and forwards
and
you wonder
what it would mean
if
there were
no clouds
at all.

TRUTH

Openings that fling
or only separate
but open;
woodpile crevices for mice to
disappear into;
doorways in and out,
shutters of our minds,
precise lenses, tree borings,
and mortar cracks,
slivers of light
confirming;
gauze partings
telling.
We seek these
patches that freshen
in
wisps
of affirmations,
instant glimpses,
tellings,
unhinged moments,
visions of what is
that persist
after they
pass through,
hurrying on
to the universalities
we know of
only
through them.

SPRING

No, I'll not write of spring
(I was ready when my trained self
interposed)
It's been done so often with buds
and blossoms
and fresh starts and meadows and
streams.
I will write of a neighbor
or a clock or a loved one or
coincidences
or precisions or something very
profound-like geometry,
(lasting poems come from such).
And as I debated this better way --
at that very time, mind you --
with clockwork precision, spring,
like some loved neighbor,
came angling into my room.

There is something to be learned from
such a thing.

THE SUDDEN UNEXPECTED

The sudden unexpected
lunges or sweeps at us,
jabs,
and occasionally touches the tip
of a nose
like a dusty moth
flying into somebody's business.
Damp, primordial swamps
loom,
even tears spill from lines to sheets,
heavy moist cloud layers
spill their water sacs,
sweat breaks and persists in wide covers.
Wetness is a hanging
and hovering.
But the dry—
unexpected.

MY HIGH SCHOOL...
JUST BEFORE DEMOLITION

Three lockers, dimpled from years of kicks,
angled along the scarred wall,and
plaster peeled away in spots
like open sores along its corridor length.

Door ajar told of classes no longer held,
broken chairs piled by the stairway,
lame desk straddling split threshold, a pennant
among debris in a corner.
This is too much! I said. Graves are not
to be splintered, opened! We do not
want corruption of what has been,
yet magnetism drew me to vacant rooms
once teeming; I began
retracing steps of another time,
my solitary walk before the crane-balls
smashed.

I was once here. These boards, now
warped with time, felt my touch
in study hall, my mind forming.
This blackboard, paunchy like my middle age,
I knew
and placed chalk across in equations.

I studied my open hand, and I heard
myself in cold concrete room,
"Nothing from without,
nothing from within."

In here, room 209,
Richard sat, before he went off to a war
he wrote about in columns
in prophecies unknown.
What had been his thought in this room
when he argued Chaucer in honors class
before he crawled into a belly turret in Italy
and died in a B-17?
My God, was he actually a gunner?
His scholar's brains, wrinkling,
used on trajectories?

I lost myself then among 2,000 seats
in cavernous auditorium, hollow;
it was not made to be so silent
and curve of balcony seemed like
a mocking smile,
sideshow doorway, one walks from stage
into the face itself.
Turning, I saw them laughing, pouring in
for rally, gridders wearing emblems, books on
laps as we cheered, held tightly for alma mater.
And I heard myself on stage during
variety show, singing,
and above the gargoyle emblem stared down
as it had before.

I have walked the gaping corridors, long
length of my own thought,
probed paper scraps behind lockers
pushed from walls.
They have suffered enough kicks; their scars
to become deeper in crumpled scrap heaps
along some highway.
Within them we stored our lives.

Alone, I listen for today, but I hear only
the echo of my footsteps,
the distant wind tumbling through
a cracked window,
and the long, quiet anguish
of a memory, throbbing
in its own death throes.

LIFELESS SPIDER IN THE FLOURESCENT FIXTURE

In the staccato light
set in
translucent porcelain
the widespread legs
in last futile moves;
no web, no need --
none else ever reached
this catacomb.

MY CAMERA

The aperture closes;
the day inside the camera
darkens into cherished silence:
the captured scenes
on the film
of my remembrance.

CEMETERY REGULATIONS,
MEMORIAL DAY

"All flowers must be in metal containers"-
so let there be no complainers-
"removed by Tuesday noon, a must."
And so we all, consigned to dust,
will await these tributes in stated hours.
The grounds crewmen would cut the flowers
in wide swaths if left another day.
Distasteful, but there's no better way
to keep Happy Acres manicured,
earth rest efficiently secured.
And let there be no tombstones
to mark the site of wasting bones;
they would interfere with maintenance
tractor mowers some days hence.

This surface based economy,
this bland scene appeals not to me.
Those beneath, in residue,
heeded not this point of view.
In life, untidy, they left heel marks,
spilled their drinks, cluttered parks,
scratched the car, in design defamed,
let weeds and daisies sprout untamed,
and building home or families,
or painting rooms, or planting trees
created little monuments.
We treasure now each evidence.

This cemetery, flat, sterile, shaven,
reflects not a proper haven
for our lifetime flowers, wildly growing;
it perpetuates only efficient mowing.

CREATIVITY

It is not fantasy
or from nothingness,
but blends and fresh
discoveries
of what we always have.

We ourselves do not create one line of poetry;
it comes instead in artistic activity
as we see truths already there --
even as we do in prayer.

HYMN

As petals open to the light
with plan and purpose stirred,
my thought can be in posture right:
receptive to God's word.

Not mere wish or idle pose,
but what sincere I do --
for just as beauty comes to the rose,
the truth uplifts my view.

My joy this day to open wide
my mind, within, above;
to grow in grace, in God abide;
to flower in God's love.

IT WAS LOVE

We called him Squirt, for
obvious reasons; yet the stray pup drew
steadily to me with wrestlings
and fetchings and other joys that grew.
I was 8 and off to school
he perched by walk as I said goodbye,
our home on the busy avenue.

Bounding back later on, I asked for him.
"Oh, some teachers—yes, two teachers—the pair
came by and asked if they might take him."
My mother's words. "They live where
a farm is big, with fields for him
to roam. They wanted to take him.
He will be much happier there."

I cursed the teachers for months; I accepted, yet
"Have them return him," I pleaded.
I had love for Squirt — what
more was ever needed?

One day, a generation later,
thinking of that house, once mine
I drove the avenue
three lanes, the horns, the tire whine,
past the site, and I thought
of Squirt and, as awareness can, the truth as last
illumined the whole design.

And I knew only that day—the loss.
My mother thought farm and field would separate
the truth, the kind you cannot
accept at all when you are 8.

I cursed again, now the cars that would
not stop, and wrestled my pup again, my
arms so full of him, my mother's
hesitant words, her attempt awry.
But it was all love, of course. The pup, the words.
And the growing up. And looking out.
All to verify.

DO THEY DREAM?

Do they dream?
Do they see in thought beyond
the gnarled rope that
defines their lives?

I see the collies, shepherd,
and, more, the nameless breed
in endless circles around
some backyard shelter.
Entire lives in an 8-foot world.
And, at times, after the long
sounds, the pleadings, the
thrusts against the chain,
then the silent starings across
fields, groves, streets,
rise of land.

Do they dream?
Do they think of more?
Do they range in wider sphere
than ever their owners know?

FLYING MODEL AIRPLANES

Counting was important.
Some took 75 turns,
others as much as 500,
set by bulkheads, stringers,
type of rubber band.

I held the fuselage
and looked in the cockpit eye,
dreaming of rudder pedals
and bank indicators, RPM,
as I cranked the balsa
propeller, felt it tighten
against my forefinger.
Each turn I gave
meant one more upward
leap
for the model airplane
and, just as well,
for the sky-filled realm
of my heart.

TELLING

There are some things every day
that we so much want to say
(concerning heart, soul, humanity,
life and love and eternity)
but if we try to share such thought
it's difficult to convey, and not
come up with something which, though definite,
is sadly just the opposite.
And little flecks of thoughts enshroud
whatever phrases were allowed;
remnants of what we had in mind
that float for others still to find.

WASHINGTON, FEBRUARY

Wind brittled cold
pushed through my coat
even to fingers huddled
within furred gloves.

I thought of how,
at worst,
it would be
if, without gloves,
I could only thrust
bare hands into the sleek
coat pockets.
Shuddering at the thought,
I saw a man
against the corner swirls
hunch, eyes slitted against
that wind,
and pole himself on.

He had neither left leg
nor gloves at all
and his fingers gritted
metal
crutch bars.

SIDEWALKS

Although the street itself
arrows in straight course,
the sidewalks
on Wellesley Drive
(in Albuquerque, where
the Rio Grande moves)
are in crooked hesitant lines.
Trees, sprouted before concrete came
to the valley,
take precedence! The walks
veer and jump aside for them!
I like all of this,
the open circles in the walks,
tribute to priorities given.
West of Albuquerque
the Rio Grande
weaves its welcome way
pausing, too, for bend and sway.

MEETING THE LECTURER

She spoke first:
"So wonderful to see you again!"

Puzzled, I thought
this stranger spoke of me,
but her eyes were above
in cold early morning
as the train and throng
moved on.

Duty had sent me;
I had her name, nothing more.

"There is my sun!"
She spoke such an intimacy
as though I had always known her.
Then, confiding further,
"He was with me
last evening, you know,
when I left."

Though her eyes and mine
had not yet met,
brightness surrounded
as I nodded to her,
to this dear, long-time friend
who, in that crowd of dull intentions,
had claimed the new sun's goodness
as her own --
and shared it
freely.

I CLOSE THE GATE

By the backyard fence
my hand moves to close the gate,
but there is no need this day
for he is gone.
The yard, his territory,
the trees and grass and plantings
and the bird feeder to be checked,
the little mesa where he rolled in the sun.
It was love
that closed the gate
making sure
against the busy street in front,
the daily flurry racing by
and love is here
though he is gone,
my little dog, my Sunny.

I am here now
not in idle ritual, but
in love's endeavor,
and start to close the gate.
Above, summer sky blankets us,
he now part of backyard soil,
I at the gate.

There is no need now, yet
love moves my hand,
making sure.

THEY ARE

They are, of course,

and because they are there is the
meaning.
If one did not use absurdities
there would be only
the nod, the smile, the
know what I mean?
If one remains at third
there is no try and the try
is what brings the absurd to
home.
It is why we prefer home.
If there is no try what is home
without the try?
The show? The game?

What if there is none?

It is better that they are.

Lyle Crist is a Professor of English and Journalism at Mount Union College in Alliance, Ohio. His previous books include two texts on writing, a biography of deaf-blind Dr. Richard Kinney, and a collection of his poetry.

He is on the lecture circuit nationwide giving programs of humor and of creative insight and communication skills ... and he occasionally risks and runs.